Advertising Fundamentals Q&A

by

Pinnacle Press

I0465434

ADVERTISING
FUNDAMENTALS

Q&A

PINNACLE PRESS

Introduction

Effective advertising is more crucial than ever in today's highly competitive marketplace. Understanding the fundamentals of advertising is essential for success. "Advertising Fundamentals Q&A," provides you with the core concepts, strategies, and best practices in the advertising industry. Structured in a question-and-answer format, it is a guide that helps you easily understand the core concepts of this topic.

Whether you are looking to start your career in advertising, enhance your skills, a business owner or simply want to know how advertising works, this book can guide you to better understand the fundamentals of advertising.

Enjoy the read!

Table of Contents

Chapter 1: Introduction to Advertising

1. What is advertising, and why is it important?

Advertising is the process of creating and delivering persuasive messages to promote a product, service, or brand.

2. Does advertising help consumers?

Yes, advertising helps consumers.

3. How does advertising help consumers?

Advertising can help consumers make informed choices before buying a product.

4. What are the primary goals of advertising?

The primary goals of advertising are brand awareness, lead generation, sales conversion, customer retention, and market positioning.

5. What is brand awareness?

Brand awareness is building recognition and familiarity with a brand.

6. What is lead generation?

Lead generation is getting people interested in a product or service so they ask for more information or show interest.

7. What is sales conversion?

Sales conversion is persuading consumers to make a purchase or take a specific action, such as signing up for a newsletter.

8. What is customer retention?

Customer retention is engaging existing customers to encourage repeat purchases and build brand loyalty.

9. What is market positioning?

Market positioning is establishing a brand's identity and distinguishing it from competitors in the marketplace.

10. What is the role of creativity in advertising?

Creativity is the key to effective advertising. A compelling ad needs to catch attention, invoke emotions, and connect with the audience.

11. How do advertisers decide on the most effective message to communicate?

To determine the most effective message to communicate, advertisers must first understand their target audience. Advertisers conduct market research to gather insights about consumer preferences, behaviors, and pain points. Advertisers then create messages that align with the audience's values and aspirations, ensuring that the message is not only clear but also emotionally impactful.

12. What are the common types of advertising?

The common types of advertising are print advertising, broadcast advertising, outdoor advertising, digital advertising, influencer advertising, and native advertising.

13. What is print advertising?

Print advertising includes newspapers, magazines, brochures, and flyers.

14. What is broadcast advertising?

Broadcast advertising includes television and radio commercials.

15. What is outdoor advertising?

Outdoor advertising includes billboards, transit ads, and posters in public spaces.

16. What is digital advertising?

Digital advertising includes online ads, social media promotions, and search engine marketing.

17. What is influencer advertising?

Influencer advertising includes collaborations with social media influencers to promote products.

18. What is native advertising?

Native advertising includes sponsored content that matches the style and format of the platform where it appears.

Chapter 2: Understanding the Audience

1. Who is the target audience?

The target audience refers to a specific group of consumers that a brand aims to reach with its advertising efforts.

2. How do you define the target audience?

Defining the target audience involves identifying demographic, psychographic, and behavioral characteristics, such as age, gender, income, education, interests, and purchasing habits.

3. What methods can be used to research and understand your audience?

Methods that can be used to research and understand your audience include surveys and questionnaires, focus groups, social media analytics, website analytics, market research reports, and customer feedback.

4. What are surveys and questionnaires?

Surveys and questionnaires are tools that collect direct feedback from potential customers regarding their preferences, needs, and behaviors.

5. What are focus groups?

Focus groups are small groups of people engaging in discussions about a product or brand, providing qualitative insights into consumer perceptions and motivations.

6. What is Social media analytics?

Social media analytics involves analyzing engagement metrics and audience demographics on social media platforms which reveals valuable information about audience interests and behaviors.

7. What is website analytics?

Website analytics helps track visitor behavior on a website, revealing what content connects most with users and how they navigate the site.

8. What are market research reports?

Market research reports are industry reports that provide insights into market trends, competitive analysis, and consumer behavior patterns.

9. How do consumer behaviors influence advertising strategies?

Consumer behaviors influence advertising strategies by buying patterns, media consumption, response to messaging, trends and preferences, and brand loyalty.

10. How do buying patterns influence advertising strategies?

Knowing when and how often consumers make purchase can help determine the timing and frequency of advertising campaigns.

11. How does media consumption influence advertising strategies?

Knowing which channels, such as social media, television, or print, the target audience prefers allows advertisers to allocate their budgets more effectively and reach consumers where they are most active.

12. How does response to messaging influence advertising strategies?

Analyzing how different audience segments respond to various types of messaging can guide advertisers in creating messages that are more likely to connect with their intended audience.

13. How do trends and preferences influence advertising strategies?

Keeping track of evolving consumer trends and preferences ensures that advertising remains relevant and appealing.

14. How does brand loyalty influence advertising strategies?

Understanding factors that contribute to brand loyalty can help advertisers develop strategies to retain customers and encourage repeat purchases.

15. What are psychographics?

Psychographics are the psychological attributes of consumers, including their values, beliefs, lifestyles, and interests. Psychographics go beyond demographic data to provide a deeper understanding of why consumers behave the way they do.

16. Why are psychographics important in advertising?

Psychographics are important in advertising because they allow marketers to create more personalized and relevant messages that connect with the emotional and psychological needs of the audience. By understanding what motivates consumers, advertisers can build stronger connections and drive engagement.

17. What is segmentation?

Segmentation is breaking down a large target audience into smaller, specific groups based on certain characteristics.

18. How can segmentation improve advertising effectiveness?

Segmentation improves advertising effectiveness in several ways:

Personalization: Creating messages for different groups makes ads more relevant and meaningful to each group.
Efficient Resource Use: Advertisers can focus their efforts on groups more likely to respond, getting better results from their budget.
Clearer Positioning: Segmentation helps define the brand's place in the market, making it stand out from competitors.

Better Engagement: By focusing on the specific needs of each group, advertisers can create more interesting campaigns that encourage people to interact and stay loyal.

19. What are customer personas?

Customer personas are detailed profiles of ideal customers created using data and research. They help businesses understand who their target customers are.

20. What tools can advertisers use to create customer personas?

Advertisers can use the following tools to create customer personas:

Surveys and Interviews: Talk directly to customers to learn about their needs and interests.

Data Analytics Tools: Tools like Google Analytics and social media insights give information on customer age, location, and behavior.

Customer Relationship Management (CRM) Systems: CRM tools store customer data, helping advertisers see buying habits and preferences.

Persona Templates: Many websites offer templates to help advertisers build customer profiles.

Competitor Analysis: Looking at competitors' audiences can give ideas about possible customer groups.

Chapter 3: Advertising Channels

1. What are advertising channels?

Advertising channels are the platforms and mediums through which advertisers communicate their messages to their target audience.

2. What are the primary types of advertising channels?

The primary types of advertising channels are:

Traditional Media

Print Advertising: Includes ads in newspapers, magazines, brochures, and flyers.
Broadcast Advertising: Commercials on television and radio.
Outdoor Advertising: Ads on billboards, posters, and public transportation.

Digital Media

Social Media Advertising: Ads on platforms like Facebook, Instagram, Twitter, and LinkedIn, targeting users based on their interests and demographics.
Search Engine Marketing (SEM): Paid ads on search engine results pages, mainly through pay-per-click (PPC) campaigns.
Display Advertising: Visual ads shown on websites and apps, often in banner or sidebar spots.

Content Marketing

Sponsored Content: Articles, videos, or blog posts featuring a product or service.
Influencer Marketing: Partnerships with social media influencers to promote products to their followers.

Email Marketing

Direct outreach to potential and existing customers through emails, newsletters, and promotions.

Native Advertising

Ads designed to blend in with the platform's style and function.

3. How do traditional media (TV, radio, print) compare to digital media?

Traditional and digital media each have unique strengths and weaknesses:

Each has its own strengths and weaknesses:

Reach

Traditional Media: TV and radio can quickly reach large audiences, making them good for building brand awareness.
Digital Media: Allows precise targeting, so advertisers can reach specific groups based on age, interests, and online activity.

Engagement

Traditional Media: Limited interaction, as there are no ways to directly respond.
Digital Media: Encourages engagement through likes, shares, comments, and messages, enabling real-time interaction and feedback.

Cost

Traditional Media: Can be more expensive, especially for prime TV slots or big publications.
Digital Media: Usually more affordable, with flexible budgets to fit businesses of all sizes.
Measurement
Traditional Media: Harder to measure effectiveness, relying on estimates and surveys.

Digital Media: Provides detailed analytics, tracking results in real-time, like clicks, conversions, and ROI.

4. What role do social media platforms play in advertising?

Social media platforms have transformed the advertising world by providing businesses with unique opportunities to connect with audiences. Their roles include:

Targeted Advertising: Advertisers can target specific demographics, interests, and behaviors, ensuring that messages reach the most relevant audience segments.

Engagement and Interaction: Social media allows for two-way communication, enabling brands to engage with consumers directly, respond to inquiries, and gather feedback.

Content Sharing: Users can share content easily, increasing the possibility for organic reach and word-of-mouth promotion.

Influencer Partnerships: Collaborating with influencers can strengthen brand messages and build on their established trust with followers.

Real-Time Insights: Advertisers can monitor engagement metrics and audience feedback in real time, allowing for quick modifications to campaigns based on performance.

5. How do advertisers choose the right channel for their campaigns?

Advertisers choose the right channel for their campaigns by considering their:

Target Audience: Understanding where the target audience spends their time and what platforms they engage with most frequently is crucial for channel selection.

Campaign Goals: Different channels serve different purposes. For instance, if the goal is brand awareness, broader channels like TV or outdoor advertising may be appropriate, while direct response campaigns may benefit from digital channels.

Budget: Advertisers must consider their budget constraints and choose channels that align with their financial resources. Digital channels often provide more flexible pricing options.

Content Type: The nature of the advertising content can influence the channel choice. For example, visually rich content may perform better on platforms like Instagram, while informative content may be more suited for blogs or newsletters.

Measurability: Some channels offer more robust analytics than others. Advertisers should consider how important it is to measure campaign effectiveness when selecting channels.

6. What are the benefits of a multi-channel advertising approach?

The benefits of a multi-channel advertising approach are:

Increased Reach: Engaging with consumers across multiple platforms boosts visibility and increases the chances of reaching a wider audience.

Reinforced Messaging: Consistent messaging across various channels helps strengthen brand identity and makes it easier for consumers to remember the brand.

Better Targeting: Different channels attract different audience segments, allowing advertisers to target diverse demographics and increase engagement.

Improved Performance: Multi-channel campaigns often yield higher overall results, as they create multiple opportunities for consumers to interact with the brand.

Flexibility: If one channel doesn't perform well, others can compensate, ensuring that advertising efforts are more resilient and adaptable.

Chapter 4: The Creative Process

1. What are the key components of an effective advertisement?

The key components of an effective advertisement include the following:

Attention-Grabbing Headline: The headline is the first thing a potential customer sees. It should be catchy, clear, and compelling enough to draw attention and encourage further reading.

Engaging Visuals: Strong visuals (images, graphics, videos) can trigger emotions and communicate messages quickly. They should be relevant to the product and connect with the target audience.

Clear Message: The advertisement should communicate a clear and concise message about the product or service, including its benefits and features. Avoid complex language and focus on language that is easy to understand.

Unique Selling Proposition (USP): The USP highlights what makes the product or service different from competitors. It should answer the question: "Why should consumers choose this product over others?"

Call to Action (CTA): A strong CTA encourages the audience to take immediate action, whether it's making a purchase, signing up for a newsletter, or visiting a website. Phrases like "Buy Now" or "Learn More" are effective examples.

Branding Elements: Consistent use of branding elements, such as logos, colors, and fonts, helps reinforce brand identity and ensures recognition across different channels.

2. How do you develop a unique selling proposition (USP)?

Here are several steps in developing a Unique Selling Proposition (USP):

Research the Competition: Analyze competitors to identify their strengths and weaknesses. This helps determine what they offer and where your product can stand out.

Understand Customer Needs: Gather insights into what customers value most in a product or service. This can involve surveys, focus groups, or social media engagement.

Identify Product Benefits: List the benefits of your product that fulfill customer needs. Focus on features that provide real value and solve specific problems.

Find the Unique Angle: Determine what differentiates your product from others in the market. This could be based on quality, price, features, customer service, or brand story.

Craft a Clear Statement: Write a succinct statement that encapsulates the essence of your USP. Ensure it is memorable and easily understood.

Test and Refine: Test your USP with a sample audience to assess its effectiveness. Be open to feedback and willing to make changes as necessary.

3. What is the role of storytelling in advertising?

The role of storytelling in advertising is creating emotional connections between the brand and its audience.

4. Is storytelling effective? If so, why?

Yes. Storytelling is effective. Here are some reasons why storytelling is effective:

Emotional Engagement: Stories invoke emotions, making the audience more likely to remember the message and feel a connection to the brand.

Relatability: A well-crafted story can connect with consumers' experiences, making the advertisement feel more personal and relevant.

Memorability: Stories are often more memorable than facts or figures alone. A narrative helps reinforce the brand message and ensures it stays in the audience's mind.

Brand Identity: Storytelling can help establish a brand's personality and values, differentiating it from competitors and building loyalty.

Inspiration and Aspiration: Stories can inspire and motivate consumers by illustrating how a product or service can improve their lives or solve their problems.

5. How do you brainstorm creative ideas for advertising campaigns?

To brainstorm creative ideas for advertising campaigns, you can use several techniques:

Mind Mapping: Start with a central idea (the product or campaign goal) and create a visual map of related ideas, concepts, and themes to study connections.

Free Writing: Set a timer and write down all ideas that come to mind without filtering. This exercise can lead to unexpected and original concepts.

Role Playing: Have team members assume different roles (e.g., customer, competitor, industry expert) to gain various perspectives and generate ideas based on different viewpoints.

Brainstorming Sessions: Gather a diverse group of individuals to share ideas in an open and collaborative environment. Encourage all participants to contribute without judgment.

Creative Prompts: Use prompts or challenges (e.g., "How would you sell this product to a child?") to stimulate out-of-the-box thinking.

Inspiration Boards: Collect images, quotes, and examples of other successful ads that inspire creativity. This visual stimulation can spark new ideas.

6. What is the importance of testing and feedback in the creative process?

The importance of testing and feedback in the creative process are:

Refinement of Ideas: Gathering feedback helps identify strengths and weaknesses in advertising concepts, allowing for refinement before the final launch.

Audience Insights: Testing ads with real audiences provides valuable insights into how the target market responds, ensuring the message connects effectively.

Risk Reduction: Testing allows advertisers to identify potential issues and make changes, reducing the risk of launching an ineffective or poorly received campaign.

Measuring Effectiveness: Analyzing test results helps determine which elements of the campaign work best, guiding future advertising strategies.

Continuous Improvement: Feedback creates opportunities for learning and growth, enabling advertisers to develop more effective campaigns over time.

Chapter 5: Advertising Strategies

1. What are the different types of advertising strategies?

The different types of advertising strategies are:

Brand Awareness Strategy
Goal: Build recognition and familiarity with the brand among potential customers.
Approach: Uses broad channels like TV, radio, and digital ads to increase visibility.

Direct Response Strategy
Goal: Encourage immediate action from consumers, like a purchase, sign-up, or website visit.
Approach: Features clear calls to action and works well with email marketing, PPC ads, and social media.

Content Marketing Strategy
Goal: Provide valuable content that attracts and engages the target audience.
Approach: Includes blog posts, videos, infographics, and social media posts that educate and inform rather than sell directly.

Influencer Marketing Strategy
Goal: Leverage influencers' trust and authority to promote products or services to their followers.
Approach: Uses individuals with strong online presences to endorse the brand.

Seasonal or Event-based Strategy
Goal: Tie promotions to holidays, seasons, or events, making them timely and relevant.
Approach: Invokes emotions associated with specific times, creating urgency and relevance.

Social Media Strategy
Goal: Use social media to build brand awareness, engage with customers, and drive conversions.

Approach: Tailors content to each platform and actively engages with followers through comments, messages, and shares.

2. How can businesses decide which strategy to use?

Businesses can decide which strategy to use by:

Target Audience
Understanding your audience is essential, including their age, interests, and behaviors. For example, younger audiences often respond better to social media campaigns than traditional media.

Campaign Goals
Establishing clear objectives such as brand awareness, lead generation, or sales conversions helps in selecting strategies that align closely with these goals.

Budget
The available budget can influence the choice of strategy. Some options, like influencer marketing or digital ads, provide more affordable, scalable choices for businesses with limited budgets.

Market Research
Analyzing competitors and industry trends can reveal effective strategies within your market. This research offers insights into approaches that connect with your target audience.

Testing and Flexibility
Starting with a variety of strategies and monitoring their performance is beneficial. Flexibility and readiness to adapt based on results help maximize effectiveness.

3. What is the importance of a multi-channel approach?

The importance of a multi-channel approach includes:

Increased Reach: Engaging consumers across multiple platforms ensures that advertisements are seen by a broader audience, increasing the likelihood of reaching potential customers.

Reinforcement of Brand Message: Consistent messaging across channels reinforces brand identity and improves message retention. When consumers see the same message in different places, it enhances recall.

Diverse Engagement: Different audience segments may prefer different channels. A multi-channel approach allows advertisers to engage with various demographics effectively.

Better Performance Metrics: By analyzing performance across multiple channels, advertisers can identify which platforms yield the best results and adjust their strategies accordingly.

Resilience: If one channel underperforms, others can compensate, making the overall campaign more resilient and effective.

4. What is segmentation?

Segmentation is dividing a broad target audience into smaller, more defined groups based on specific characteristics.

5. What are the benefits of segmentation?

The benefits of segmentation include:

Personalized Messaging: Tailored messages for each segment increase relevance and connect more deeply with consumers, improving engagement and conversion rates.

Improved Targeting: Advertisers can allocate resources more effectively by focusing on segments that are more likely to convert, leading to a higher return on investment.

Enhanced Understanding of Audience Needs: Segmentation allows advertisers to understand the unique needs and preferences of different groups, enabling more targeted product offerings.

Strategic Resource Allocation: By identifying the most profitable segments, businesses can prioritize their advertising budgets and efforts accordingly.

Clear Positioning: Segmentation helps clarify the brand's position in the market, making it easier to differentiate from competitors and communicate effectively with specific audience groups.

6. What are some common pitfalls in advertising strategy?

Some common pitfalls in the advertising strategy include:

Lack of Clear Objectives: Without defined goals, it can be challenging to measure the success of a campaign or determine the right strategies to implement.

Ignoring the Target Audience: Failing to understand the audience can lead to ineffective messaging and poor engagement. Researching and defining the target audience is crucial.

Overlooking Testing and Feedback: Launching campaigns without testing them fully can lead to costly mistakes. Gathering feedback is essential for refining strategies and improving performance.

Inconsistent Branding: Inconsistency across channels can confuse consumers and dilute brand identity. Maintaining a cohesive brand image is vital for recognition and trust.

Neglecting Analytics: Ignoring data and performance metrics can hinder a business's ability to optimize campaigns and make informed decisions.

Chapter 6: Measuring Success

1. How do you define success in advertising?

Success in advertising can be defined by Lead Generation, Sales Conversion, Customer Engagement, and Return on Investment (ROI).

2. What is Lead Generation?

Lead Generation is the number of inquiries, sign-ups, or downloads generated by an advertising campaign.

3. What is Sales Conversion?

Sales Conversion is the number of sales or transactions resulting from the campaign.

4. What is Customer Engagement?

Customer Engagement are metrics like social media interactions (likes, shares, comments), website traffic, and email open rates. These metrics reflect how well the audience is engaging with the advertising content.

5. What is ROI?

Return on Investment (ROI) is comparing the revenue generated from the advertising campaign against the costs incurred. A positive ROI indicates that the campaign was successful in generating profit.

6. What metrics are important for evaluating advertising effectiveness?

The metrics that are important for evaluating advertising effectiveness are Reach and Impressions, Click-Through Rate (CTR), Conversion Rate, Cost Per Acquisition (CPA), Customer Lifetime Value (CLV), and Engagement Metrics.

7. What is Reach?

Reach indicates the total number of unique individuals who saw the advertisement.

8. What are impressions?

Impressions measure how many times the ad was displayed.

9. What is Click-Through Rate (CTR)?

Click-Through Rate (CTR) is the percentage of users who clicked on the advertisement after seeing it.

10. What is Conversion Rate?

Conversion Rate is the percentage of users who completed a desired action (e.g., making a purchase, signing up) after interacting with the advertisement.

11. What is Cost Per Acquisition?

Cost Per Acquisition (CPA) is the total cost of acquiring a customer through the advertising campaign.

12. What is Customer Lifetime Value (CLV)?

Customer Lifetime Value (CLV) is an estimate of the total revenue a business can expect from a single customer throughout their relationship.

13. What is A/B testing?

A/B testing is a method used to compare two or more variations of an advertisement to determine which performs better.

14. A/B testing is also known as?

A/B testing is also known as split testing

15. How can A/B testing improve advertising results?

A/B testing can improve advertising results by Data-Driven Decisions, Optimizing Elements, Improving ROI, Reducing Risks, and Understanding Audience Preferences.

16. How do Data-Driven Decisions improve advertising results?

Data-Driven Decisions, like those from A/B testing, provide concrete data on how different ad elements (e.g., headlines, visuals, CTAs) perform, allowing advertisers to make informed choices based on actual results.

17. How do Optimizing Elements improve advertising results?

Optimizing Elements such as testing variations of headlines, images, and ad placements helps advertisers identify which elements connect best with their audience, optimizing the ad for higher engagement and conversions.

18. How does Improving ROI improve advertising results?

Continually refining ads through A/B testing enhance campaign effectiveness, leading to better results and higher return on ad spend.

19. How does Reducing Risks improve advertising results?

Testing variations in advance minimizes the risk of launching an ineffective campaign, allowing advertisers to validate concepts and messaging before significant investment.

20. What tools are available for measuring advertising performance?

Tools such as Google Analytics, Social Media Analytics Tools, Email Marketing Software, A/B Testing Platforms, Customer Relationship Management (CRM) Systems, and Advertising Platforms.

Chapter 7: Ethics in Advertising

1. What ethical considerations should advertisers keep in mind?

Ethical considerations that advertisers should keep in mind include Truthfulness, Transparency, Respect for Privacy, Avoiding Stereotypes, Social Responsibility, and Compliance and Regulations.

2. What is Truthfulness for Advertisers?

Truthfulness for Advertisers means that Advertisers must ensure that all claims made in advertisements are truthful and not misleading. This includes providing accurate information about products, services, and pricing.

3. What is Transparency for Advertisers?

Transparency for Advertisers means that Advertisers should disclose any material information that could affect a consumer's decision. This includes sponsorship disclosures in influencer marketing and clarity regarding terms and conditions.

4. What is Respect for Privacy for Advertisers?

Respect for Privacy for Advertisers means that Advertisers must respect consumer privacy by obtaining consent for data collection and ensuring secure handling of personal information.

5. What is Social Responsibility for Advertisers?

Social Responsibility for Advertisers means that Advertisers should consider the possible societal impact of their messages and avoid promoting harmful behaviors, such as substance abuse or unhealthy lifestyles.

6. What is Compliance with Regulations for Advertisers?

Compliance with Regulations for Advertisers means that Advertisers must adhere to all relevant laws and regulations governing advertising practices, such as truth-in-advertising laws and specific industry guidelines.

7. What role does consumer feedback play in promoting ethical advertising?

Consumer feedback is essential for promoting ethical advertising practices by:

Highlighting Concerns: Feedback from consumers can reveal possible ethical issues or concerns with advertisements, prompting brands to make necessary changes.

Encouraging Accountability: When consumers hold brands accountable for their advertising practices, it promotes a culture of responsibility and encourages companies to prioritize ethics.

Shaping Brand Reputation: Positive consumer feedback regarding ethical practices can enhance a brand's reputation, while negative feedback can lead to public backlash and harm brand trust.

Guiding Future Campaigns: Consumer insights can inform future advertising strategies, helping brands understand what connects positively with audiences and what should be avoided.

Building Relationships: Engaging with consumers and responding to their feedback builds trust and loyalty, demonstrating that the brand values their opinions and is committed to ethical practices.

Chapter 8: The Future of Advertising

1. How is technology influencing the future of advertising?

Technology is influencing the future of advertising in several ways such as Data-Driven Marketing, Programmatic Advertising, Artificial Intelligence (AI), Augmented Reality (AR), Virtual (VR), Voice Search and Smart Speakers, and Social Media Innovations.

2. How does Data-Driven Marketing enhance the effectiveness of advertising strategies?

Advances in data analytics allow advertisers to collect and analyze large amounts of consumer data, enabling more targeted and personalized advertising strategies. By understanding consumer behavior, preferences, and trends, advertisers can create messages that relates more deeply with their audiences.

3. How does Programmatic Advertising improve ad placements?

Programmatic Advertising automates the buying and selling of ads in real-time, optimizing placements based on data to efficiently reach specific audiences across multiple platforms.

4. How is Artificial Intelligence (AI) used in advertising?

AI analyzes consumer data, predicts trends, and personalizes ad experiences. It powers chatbots, optimizes ad placements, and boosts campaign efficiency and effectiveness.

5. How do Augmented Reality (AR) and Virtual Reality (VR) enhance consumer engagement?

AR and VR offer immersive experiences, allowing consumers to try products virtually, like clothing or furniture, before purchasing, creating deeper brand engagement.

6. How does Voice Search impact advertising strategies?

With the rise of voice-activated devices, advertisers need to optimize content for voice search and consider reaching consumers through platforms like Amazon Alexa and Google Assistant.

7. How do Social Media Innovations help advertisers engage audiences?

New features like shoppable posts, stories, and live streaming allow advertisers to engage directly with audiences, encouraging interaction and immediate purchasing decisions.

8. What trends are emerging in the advertising industry?

Trends emerging in the advertising industry include a focus on personalization, sustainability, short-form video content, evolving influencer marketing, privacy and data protection, and experiential marketing. These trends reflect a shift towards more targeted, ethical, and engaging advertising strategies.

9. How can businesses prepare for changes in consumer behavior and technology?

Businesses can prepare by welcoming innovation, investing in data analytics, prioritizing customer experience, staying flexible, enhancing collaboration across departments, and monitoring consumer trends to stay relevant and responsive.

10. What role do ethical considerations play in the future of advertising?

Ethical considerations are essential for building consumer trust, protecting brand reputation, promoting sustainability, encouraging diversity and inclusion, and ensuring regulatory compliance. These factors will shape the future of advertising.

11. How can businesses leverage emerging technologies while maintaining ethical advertising practices?

To use emerging technologies ethically, businesses should prioritize transparency, secure consumer data, adopt inclusive practices, evaluate technology impacts, and provide ethical training to ensure responsible advertising practices.

Chapter 9: Getting Started in Advertising

1. What skills are essential for a career in advertising?

Essential skills for a career in advertising include creativity, communication, analytical thinking, project management, understanding marketing principles, digital literacy, and adaptability.

2. How can beginners break into the advertising industry?

Beginners can break into the advertising industry by pursuing relevant education, securing internships, building a portfolio, networking, staying informed on trends, and developing a personal brand.

3. What resources are available for ongoing learning in advertising?

Resources available for ongoing learning include online courses, industry conferences, books, webinars, professional associations, and mentorship opportunities.

4. What are the key takeaways for aspiring advertisers?

Key takeaways include incorporating creativity, being persistent, understanding industry fundamentals, networking actively, staying adaptable, and prioritizing ethical standards.

Conclusion

Understanding the fundamentals of Advertising is essential for anyone looking to succeed in this dynamic field. Throughout this book, we have examined the key principles of advertising, from defining what advertising is and its importance, to understanding the target audience, the creative process, and the various strategies that drive effective campaigns.

We've seen how technology continues to reshape the industry, enabling advertisers to connect with consumers in new and innovative ways. As we look to the future, trends such as personalization, sustainability, and the rise of digital and social media are set to play a crucial role in how brands communicate their messages.

Equally important are the ethical considerations that govern advertising practices. The responsibility to engage in truthful, transparent, and socially conscious advertising is essential for building trust with consumers and building long-term brand loyalty.

For those aspiring to enter the advertising industry, the insights shared in this book provide a solid foundation for navigating the complexities of this exciting field. Emphasizing the importance of creativity, continuous learning, and adaptability will equip future advertisers to respond to the challenges and opportunities that lie ahead.

Ultimately, successful advertising is about connecting with people, understanding their needs, emotions, and aspirations. By applying the principles and strategies discussed in this book, advertisers can create meaningful and impactful campaigns that connect with their audiences, drive engagement, and contribute to the success of their brands.

As you embark on your journey in advertising, remember to embrace creativity, uphold ethical standards, and stay curious. The world of advertising is rich with possibilities, and with the right knowledge and skills, you can make a significant impact in this constantly evolving environment.

Thank you for reading **Advertising Fundamentals Q&A**.

www.ingramcontent.com/pod-product-compliance
Lightning Source LLC
Chambersburg PA
CBHW030044230526
45472CB00005B/1670